An Anthology of Piano Music Volume I

The Baroque Period

Selected and Edited by Denes Agay

With an Introduction by Louis L. Crowder

Head of the Department of Music
The University of Connecticut

Yorktown Music Press: New York
Music Sales Limited: London

Order No. YK 20212
International Standard Book Number: 0.8256.8041.7

Exclusive Distributors:
Music Sales Corporation
257 Park Avenue South, New York, NY 10010 USA
Music Sales Limited
8/9 Frith Street, London W1V 5TZ England
Music Sales Pty. Limited
120 Rothschild Street, Rosebery, Sydney, NSW 2018, Australia

Printed in the United States of America by
Vicks Lithograph and Printing Corporation

FOREWORD

The content of AN ANTHOLOGY OF PIANO MUSIC was selected from the keyboard literature of nearly four centuries. From the early Baroque to the present, through the works of 139 composers, all important musical idioms and modes of expression are represented. The material is divided into four volumes:

Volume I — THE BAROQUE PERIOD — from the end of the 16th century (late Renaissance) to the end of the 18th (Rococo).

Volume II — THE CLASSICAL PERIOD — the second half of the 18th and the early 19th centuries. (Haydn, Mozart, Beethoven and their contemporaries.)

Volume III — THE ROMANTIC PERIOD — piano music of the 19th century.

Volume IV — THE TWENTIETH CENTURY — piano works by major composers of our time.

It is hardly necessary to point out that no rigid stylistic boundaries separate these volumes and that, inevitably, there is some chronological and idiomatic overlapping. The works of the sons of Johann Sebastian Bach, for instance, which conclude the baroque volume could have been placed as well at the beginning of the classical section. Fauré, Sibelius, Rachmaninoff and others, who wrote during the late 19th and early 20th centuries, could have been included in either the romantic or the contemporary volume, depending on whether we consider their modes of writing or their life-spans as a yardstick. It is better, then, to view this Anthology, and for that matter, the entire music literature, not as a succession of clearly separated and defined plateaus, but rather as a broad, ever-flowing stream with many branches and tributaries. This stream, the literature of keyboard music, is so vast that even the impressively sizable body of this Anthology, amounting to nearly one thousand pages, can represent but a small fraction of it.

This fact alone can give a hint of the difficult process involved in selecting the contents of these volumes and of the often thorny decisions the editor had to make. Which Preludes and Fugues of Bach's "48" should be chosen? Which Sonatas of Mozart and Beethoven should be included? Are the contributions to keyboard romanticism of an Heller or an Alkan substantial enough to warrant inclusion? Is the amount of space allocated to a certain composer in proper ratio to his importance? These and other similar questions had to be answered, always keeping in mind the main purpose of this Anthology and constantly trying to achieve a reasonable balance between the aesthetic, pedagogic, and historic considerations on the one hand and the dictates of space limitations, on the other.

The purpose of this Anthology is twofold: to present a comprehensive survey of the entire keyboard literature through works which are appealing and representative, without being too demanding from either a musical or technical point of view; and to furnish an academically sound and varied teaching and performing library. The grade level of the contents ranges from easy to advanced, with the bulk of the material falling well within the intermediate grades. We felt that this segment of the piano repertory can furnish the most suitable materials for our multi-purpose collections. For this reason, works demanding utmost musical maturity and technical virtuosity, such as the late Sonatas of Beethoven, the lengthier concert pieces of Schumann, Chopin, Liszt, and others were not included.

All selections are based on authentic sources and are in their original forms. Tempo, dynamic, and expression marks in small print or in parentheses are editorial additions and should be regarded as suggestions rather than rigid directions. In this, the baroque volume, it seemed advisable to present some very lengthy works, mostly those in variation forms, in judicially abbreviated versions. This does not necessarily violate the spirit of 17th and 18th century performance practices. Some masters of the period openly condone, indeed encourage such deletions if they are done with taste and a regard for the proper balance of tempo and mood between the sections of the composition; or, as Frescobaldi stipulates, "if you take care to fit the various sections to one another." In line with our aim to give the player an authentic as well as a practical edition, the less familiar ornamental signs, especially those of the English virginalists and the French clavecinists, were replaced by the equivalent and better known symbols of the German Baroque (J. S. Bach). There is a review of these ornamental signs and their execution on page 18 of our baroque volume. To aid the performer in avoiding the often puzzling problems involved in the recognition and correct interpretation of *long appoggiaturas,* these signs have been written out in conventional notation throughout the baroque and classical sections.

The main body of this Anthology is compiled from the music of the great masters. Included are not only their well-known repertory pieces, but also other of their representative works which are seldom found in similar collections. We have also included a number of relatively unknown, nonetheless delightful pieces by a few minor masters. These composers were perhaps not creative minds of the first magnitude but they did produce occasional works of striking beauty, especially in the smaller forms, and should be entitled to the measure of recognition offered by an anthology.

We hope to have succeeded in conveying the many factors, viewpoints and considerations which guided the selection of materials for these volumes. The final choices inevitably reflect, of course, the personal taste and didactic principles of the editor. It should be noted, however, that the process of compilation also included extensive consultations and discussions with many distinguished pianists and educators. To them, too numerous for individual mention, we express our heartfelt thanks and gratitude. In addition, we are deeply indebted to Mr. Eugene Weintraub, for his invaluable editorial help, to Mr. Herbert H. Wise, for his patience and wisdom in guiding this large publication project, and to Professor Louis L. Crowder, for his richly illuminating commentaries on the styles and performance practices of each period.

October 1970 DENES AGAY

CONTENTS

11 The Baroque Period by Louis L. Crowder
18 A Review of Baroque Ornamentation
224 Editorial Notes
225 Biographical Sketches of Composers
230 Glossary

Music

d'Anglebert, Jean Henri
69 Air Ancien *("Ou estes vous allez")* Gavotte

Bach, Carl Philipp Emanuel
210 Capriccio (D minor)
212 Sonata (D major)

Bach, Johann Sebastian
110 Fantasia (C minor)
123 French Suite No. 6 (E major) Allemande-Courante-Sarabande-Gavotte-Polonaise-Bourrée-Menuet-Gigue
108 Fugue (C major)
102 Inventio No. 3 Two-Voice Invention in D major
98 Inventio No. 13 Two-Voice Invention in A minor
100 Inventio No. 14 Two-Voice Invention in B-flat major
96 Little Prelude No. 6 (E minor) from *Six Little Preludes for Beginners at the Clavier*
114 Preludium and Fuga XI (F major) from *The Well-Tempered Clavier, Book 1*
118 Preludium and Fuga VII (E-flat major) from *The Well-Tempered Clavier, Book 2*
104 Scherzo from *Partita No. 3* (A minor)
106 Sinfonia No. 15 Three-Voice Invention in B minor

Bach, Wilhelm Friedemann
208 Polonaise

Blow, John
44 Prelude
45 Courante

Buxtehude, Dietrich
40 Allemande d'Amour from *Suite No. 6*
41 Variations on an Aria by Lully ("Rofilis")

Byrd, William
23 Galiardo
22 Pavana (The Earl of Salisbury)

Chambonnières, Jacques Champion de
68 Gigue *ou il y a un Canon*

Couperin, François
72 L'Âme-en-Peine from *Ordre No. 13*
73 Le Réveille-Matin from *Ordre No. 4*
76 Le Rossignol-en-Amour from *Ordre No. 14*
70 Les Grâces Naturèles from *Ordre No. 11*

Dandrieu, Jean Francois
86 Le Caquet
84 La Gemissante

Daquin, Louis Claude
88 La Joyeuse (Rondeau)

Durante, Francesco
166 Two Divertimenti

Fischer, Johann Kaspar Ferdinand
62 Chaconne from *Melpomene Suite*
64 Passepied from *Melpomene Suite*
65 Prelude and Fugue from *Ariadne Musica*

Frescobaldi, Girolamo
30 Aria detto Balletto

Froberger, Johann Jakob
35 Canzon
36 Suite (B minor) Allemande-Courante-Sarabande-Gigue

Gabrieli, Giovanni
21 Intonazione from *Intonazioni d'Organo*

Galuppi, Baldassare
217 Adagio from *Sonata in D major*

Gibbons, Orlando
29 Alman
28 Coranto (A Toy)

Graupner, Christoph
186 Air en Gavotte

Handel, George Frideric
140 Air and Variations ("The Harmonious Blacksmith") from *Suite No. 5* (E major)
135 Fantasia (A major)
137 Sonatina (D minor)
144 Suite No. 11 (D minor) Allemande-Courante-Sarabande-Gigue

Hurlebusch, Conrad
184 Villanella from a *Sonata in F major*

Kindermann, Johann Erasmus
39 Ballet
38 Fuga from *Harmonia Organica*

Kirnberger, Johann Philipp
218 Les Carillons
220 Sonata (G major)

Krebs, Johann Ludwig
199 Preambulum

Krieger, Johann
67 Gavotte and Bourrée from *Sechs Musicalische Partien*

Kuhnau, Johann
56 Song of the Bridesmaids from *Biblical Sonata No. 3 (Jacob's Wedding)*
54 Victory Dance and Festival from *Biblical Sonata No. 1 (The Battle between David and Goliath)*
55 Gavotte (B minor)

Leo, Leonardo
168 Toccata (C minor)

Loeillet, Jean Baptiste
177 Hornpipe

Lully, Jean Baptiste
68 Menuet

Maichelbeck, Franz Anton
207 Buffone

Marcello, Benedetto
157 Andante Maestoso from *Sonata in B-flat major*

Martini, Giovanni Battista
190 Adagio from *Sonata in G minor*

Mattheson, Johann
60 Fantasie and Menuet from *Suite in C minor*

Muffat, Gottlieb
179 Fuga Pastorella from *72 Versets and 12 Toccatas*
178 Siciliana
180 Toccata and Fugue from *72 Versets and 12 Toccatas*

Nichelmann, Christoph
204 La Tendre
205 La Gaillarde

Pachelbel, Johann
57 Fantasie
59 Fugue

Paradisi, Pietro Domenico
192 Presto (Toccata) from *Sonata in D major*

Pasquini, Bernardo
158 Four Arias

Pergolesi, Giovanni Battista
187 Sonata (G major)

Purcell, Henry
46 A New Irish Tune
47 Ground (C minor)
46 Rigadoon
51 Suite No. 4 Prelude-Alman-Courante-Saraband

Rameau, Jean Philippe
77 Fanfarinette from *Pièces de Clavecin, Book of 1731*
83 La Boiteuse from *Pièces de Clavecin, Book of 1724*
79 La Villageoise (Rondeau) from *Pièces de Clavecin, Book of 1724*
82 Sarabandes (Two) from *Pièces de Clavecin, Book of 1706*

Rathgeber, Valentin
182 Two Pieces from *Musical Pastime at the Clavier*

Scarlatti, Domenico
170 Sonata L. 388 (G major)
172 Sonata L. 497 (B-flat major)
174 Sonata L. 263 (B minor)

Scheidt, Samuel
27 Bergamasca

Seixas, Carlos
194 Toccata (C major)

Soler, Padre Antonio
196 Sonata No. 84 (D major)

Sweelinck, Jan Pieterszoon
24 Toccata

Telemann, Georg Philipp
149 Bourrée
152 Cantabile and Fugue
154 Fantasia (B minor)

150 Loure
151 Rigaudon

Tischer, Johann Nikolaus
202 Clavier Partie from *Six Easy and Pleasant Partitas for Young Beginners*

Trabacci, Giovanni Maria
34 Ricercata from *Il Secondo Libro de Ricercate*

Walther, Johann Gottfried
94 Two Choral Preludes on *Fröhlich soll mein Herze springen*

Weckmann, Matthias
33 Sarabande

Witt, Christian Friedrich
90 Passacaglia

Zipoli, Domenico
160 Sarabanda and Giga from *Suite in G minor*
162 Theme and Variations from *Partita in A minor*

THE BAROQUE PERIOD by Louis L. Crowder

About 1580 there appeared in Europe a new architecture, exciting, blatantly theatrical, and destined to dominate architectural style, especially in Central Europe, for a century and a half. In strong reaction against the austerities of the Renaissance, its exuberance burst all well-established rules and left an immense legacy of churches, palaces, even town halls. Magnificence of exterior was matched by interior richness, and by more lavish ornament, both inside and out, than had been seen in Europe before.

Like all things new it incurred the scorn of staunch adherents of the old, who soon found a name for it—"baroque". The word is believed to come from the Portuguese "barrocco", a lop-sided pearl, and to have been a contemptuous reference to the irregularly shaped plaster blobs that were an important feature of baroque wall and ceiling ornament. The name baroque has somehow remained as a label for the whole era, with reference to both architecture and art. It has, however, absolutely nothing to do with music.

The fact is that just as baroque architecture appeared, there occurred a parallel, and possibly related, revolution in musical composition and performance, a break with the past fully as decisive as that which shook the world of architecture. And since the newly evolving musical ideals dominated music for almost exactly the same period as did baroque architecture, and since both gave way at almost the same time to classical music and rococo, it has proven a great convenience to refer to "baroque" music.

In fact, no more specifically musical term for this period would have sufficed, for the violence of the baroque revolution was matched by a diversity which almost defies description in musical terms. Opera was born, the accidental offspring of a happy marriage between a group of amateurs and their complete misapprehension concerning ancient Greek music. Opera's new dramatic device, the recitative, upset all renaissance preconceptions about meter and melody, just as opera's monophonic orientation destroyed forever the absolute supremacy of polyphony.

Not that polyphony disappeared; it simply moved over to allow room for a completely new musical point of view. At first it continued to be cultivated in pseudo-renaissance fashion as a church style of composition, separated for the first time from secular music. Then, with the maturing of the concept of tonality, it evolved toward its supreme culmination in the works of Bach and Handel.

Thoroughbass, the art of extemporizing a harmonic accompaniment over a figured bass, the most characteristic baroque invention, dominated most instrumental performance throughout the era. Instrumental and vocal styles, as a matter of fact, became for the first time differentiated. Renaissance composers had always assumed that anything which could be sung could and should be played on instruments if desired, and vice versa. Now much that was played simply could not be sung. National characteristics began to emerge—even North German traits distinct from Viennese. New forms appeared—concerto, cantata, suite, even the immediate ancestor of the classical sonata, the "sonata da chiesa". In fact the stage was set for the classical era and beyond it for all the music with which we are familiar.

Altogether an amazing age, full of the wildest of contradictions, conflicting musical ideals, and limitless variety. Performances by immense vocal and instrumental groups balanced the emergence of the solo virtuoso among organists and harpsichordists. Ideals of expressiveness which seemed to foreshadow the nineteenth-century birth of romanticism existed side by side with vestiges of renaissance restraint. Perhaps most significant of all, the Baroque developed the harmonic vocabulary that was to be used by composers for the ensuing hundred and fifty years.

Each succeeding musical period, in spite of its obsession with what was then "modern", never quite forgot the Baroque. This was true even of the narcissistic 19th century. In fact the first serious revival of 18th century music can be credited to romanticists like Schumann and Mendelssohn, who immediately recognized their kinship with Bach, welcomed his music to their hearts, and proceeded to recast it in their own image. The result was the typically enthusiastic but typically un-baroque performance of the 1800's. With few exceptions most of us inherited this 19th century point of view; it was not the product of ignorance alone, or at least not always. Theodore Presser, for example, included in his editing of a collection of early music an accurate set of ornament symbols and correct explanations of their performance. But his next thought, expressed in a footnote, reassured the reader that the contemporary manner of execution, i.e., the way they were played circa 1900, was intrinsically better in reflecting a "progress" in musical taste, and that therefore it was as well to pay no attention to the out-dated, old fashioned notions of 1750.

The Search For Authenticity

A generation or more ago, the gathering clouds of authenticity in performance practice obliterated the pleasant sunshine of this laissez-faire irresponsibility. There ensued panic, traces of which still beset many an honest piano teacher. The obligation to a supposed stylistic authenticity and the fear of some anachronistic gaffe still mar for some of us the sheer joy of baroque music, with all its variety, emotional depth, and vigor.

This is a pity, and quite unnecessary. One does not have to be a scholar to grasp the more important basic principles and thereby enjoy more fully this vital music. Nor should the resulting performance sound dull or "scholarly", certainly not "unmusical". In fact, one may categorically state that whenever an adherence to an alleged historical principle leads to such unfortunate results, one may be sure that the performer either has misunderstood the principle or has applied it wrongly. *All contemporary accounts emphasize the strength, expressiveness, and sheer vitality of baroque performance.*

Happily almost all of us have recovered from the original shocking realization that most of the editions we used were full of wrong notes, wrong ornaments incorrectly explained, and deliberate alterations. Many an eminent nineteenth-century editor was also a performer, usually a pianist, and often his lack of knowledge of baroque performance was matched only by his audacity in improving on the works of baroque composers. Better editings have freed us from their misconceptions and given us at least the basis for better understanding.

Nor are we any longer terrified by the stern pronouncements of the harpsichordists that, if we must desecrate Bach by performing his music on the piano, we should at least make it sound as much as possible like the harpsichord—even, ironically, those intimate works which Bach very probably intended for the clavichord. Many, whose desire to placate history overcame their musical common sense, climbed on this stylistic bandwagon and tried manfully to avoid shading a phrase and to use only stepwise dynamic gradations.

Gradually the absurdity of this attitude has become apparent, and for a variety of reasons. Bach himself used the clavichord as well as the harpsichord, and the clavichord, one must not forget, *could* shade the nuances of a phrase as does the piano. Couperin, through his indications of tempo and mood, revealed a pseudo-romantic attitude at times, and objected vigorously to the harpsichord's shortcomings in expressive capacities. In Bach's case, moreover, the links between the music and a specific instrument were tenuous, as witness his many transcriptions of his own works. Surely some of his melodies which could not escape expressiveness when played on the cello or violin, became less expressive when played on the harpsichord only by necessity and not because Bach wished it to be so. To reverse all logic and assert, as has been done, that the melody should be played without shading on the cello because of the harpsichord's limitation, is too fatuous to require comment. One need only read Couperin or other 18th century sources to perceive contemporary thought on this score. The studied dryness that a generation ago often resulted from a spurious authenticity probably resembled real 18th century performance no more than a prune resembles a plum.

May I insert a word here in defense of the harpsichord? It had other virtues to compensate for shading—endless coloring effects, clarity, etc. And in the hands of a really great artist, of which there are few, it *can* be made to sound expressive in baroque music, usually through rubato. Furthermore, there is even an illusion of shading in the playing of the very great harpsichordists, though how they do it baffles me.

Newer Attitudes On Performance

As controversy cools and musical common sense regains the upper hand, newer attitudes seem to be replacing those of the panic period of baroque interpretation. These may perhaps be summarized as follows, with all deference to dissident opinion:

It is indeed advantageous to preserve in a piano performance all the esthetic qualities of the harpsichord that we can: brilliance, sudden dramatic changes of dynamic level or color, above all its clarity. But beyond this there is no need to perpetuate its limitations, particularly its inability to shade or to produce a prolonged crescendo. These disadvantages irked Couperin, and to assume that Bach was less musically sensitive is ridiculous. Indeed Bach's works are full of obvious attempts to counteract the shortcomings of the harpsichord.

This volume, then, is presented on the assumption that we are playing the piano as a piano, not as an imitation harpsichord. If the music demands a crescendo, the editor has no objection to its use. Shading is taken for granted, so long as it is used with discretion and taste. Editorial markings are discreet, sparing, and in small print, allowing for that peculiar joy of baroque playing, the choosing of one's own tempo and dynamic scheme.

The rhythmic ambiguities of baroque notation, most of them concerning dotted notes, which in Bach's day could mean, depending on the connotation, anything from triplets to double dots, have been resolved in our text.

Ornamentation—A Problem With A Solution

Naturally ornaments should be correctly done; fortunately they are no more difficult done correctly than incorrectly. The familiar Bach symbols are used throughout, in the interest of easier reading. One should mention, however, that really fascinating aspect of Baroque, the latitude of personalized notation. Composers seem rarely to have used precisely the same symbols for ornaments. And the performance of even the most familiar of them was apparently a pseudo-improvisational art and subject to occasional personal variation.

The baroque trill, for example, short or long, which has been the subject of the most unpleasant controversy, has even now, after our finally correcting a century of improper performance, never been proven to have *always* and inflexibly started on the upper note, as all the late-baroque rules insist. Aside from its being slurred to the preceding note of a descending melody line and thus resulting in three notes instead of four, a fact which Couperin explains and Bach implies, there is the question of its occasional use in the manner later named and explained by C. P. E. Bach as the "schneller" and usually called more recently the "upper mordent", "inverted mordent" or "snap". There should be no doubt that the three-note schneller, starting on the principal note, existed in Germany before C. P. E. gave it a name and a new notation. In fact, in the late 16th century some of the earliest accounts of ornamentation, Italian and Spanish, describe all trills, short or long, as starting on the principal note. The situation is hardly clarified when one learns that Reinken and Murschhauser, both Germans and though older than Bach, still living during his lifetime, started all their trills on the principal note!

At this point the conscientious piano teacher can be forgiven for throwing up his hands and deciding that since everything seems to have been permitted, we may as well revert to the nonchalance of the nineteenth century and simply do whatever we please. This enticing path leads nowhere. A better solution is to understand at least the customary manner of performing the ornaments and then to allow oneself the luxury of occasional deviation whenever one's musical conviction is strong enough to justify it. Every good musician has indeed the obligation to know the rules before breaking them. With this in mind we are adding a review of the most frequently occurring ornamental signs, including their execution. This review avoids all subtleties but should, with a half hour of study, help to avoid the more common uncertainties.

This Anthology

As for the contents of this volume, some pieces are among the best known and most widely used. Along with these, however, are many others by comparative strangers whose acquaintance will be most rewarding. The variety in style and musical texture is startling. Between Couperin and Bach, for example, there is an immense distance, musical, philosophical, and stylistic. Muffat, a German composer well acquainted with French music, shows an interesting blend of the two points of view. The Spaniards, led by Scarlatti, and including his Portuguese pupil Seixas, are utterly different from the rest of Europe, through geographical and cultural isolation. Bukofzer says of Spain that "Here we have one of the very few examples of baroque music in which the influence of folk music is more than mere wishful thinking".

Relatively unknown are pieces by some of the English composers of the very early Baroque, with which the volume opens. This music, in spite of its echoes of Renaissance modality, indicates trends that would lead to the flowering of keyboard music in other lands. Both the French and the Germans were indebted to these pioneers in the composing of strictly keyboard pieces.

Representative pieces by Gabrieli, Trabacci, Frescobaldi, Pasquini and others give a fresh and illuminating glimpse of that all-but-forgotten early Italian school of keyboard composition, which has been neglected even in Italy, probably because of the Italian preoccupation with opera.

Another neglected group is represented by Telemann, Krebs, Tischer and others active toward the close of the era. In the mid-1700's the discipline and intellectuality of the high-Baroque relaxed in the pleasant, more suave, less formal music of the Rococo. (Even earlier, Couperin had stated frankly that his music was intended to please.) Here, side by side with the stately culmination of Baroque in Bach and Handel, we find developing an entertaining, often non-polyphonic keyboard music parallel to the vocal music of the time—a music suitable to the tastes of courtiers and their ladies, less demanding technically but full of the charm that justifies its name: the "gallant style".

In Germany meanwhile the declining Baroque produced a brief but powerful preview of Romanticism. Fed by literature and expressing itself through the sensitive clavichord, this second post-Baroque manifestation was quite different from the Rococo. Called "Sturm und Drang" ("Storm and Drive") and continually concerned with "Empfindsamkeit" (sensitivity), it deliberately exploited emotion, sudden dramatic contrast, and a rather exaggerated sentimentality. Bach's sons were among the leaders of this group, and as the piano superceded both harpsichord and clavichord, they helped open the way both to Classicism, and by a sort of historical leap-frog to Romanticism as well.

How To Approach Baroque Music

First, I feel I should express briefly a personal conviction based on childhood unhappiness, shared I am sure with many other youngsters. My first contact with baroque and with polyphony was through Bach's Two-Part Inventions. Granted that these are masterworks of their type, and full of charm for the discerning, they were totally inappropriate for me when I first met them head-on. I was, quite simply, not up to them. Although I could rattle off fairly impressive little pieces, full of runs and sound, those two independent lines, innocent though they looked, were beyond me intellectually, technically, and musically.

The mistake, I later discovered, was my teacher's and not a matter of my inadequacy. But for several years I nourished a grudge against Bach; it was a real surprise when I ultimately discovered that he didn't deserve it. The same sort of mistake in timing, for that was all it was, continues to be made through generation after generation of piano students.

If one prefers to begin polyphonic study with Bach, one should at least start with the Little Preludes. A still better solution is to introduce polyphony through works by various other composers who have left delightful pieces, easier than the Little Preludes and full of charm for beginning students of any age. This volume contains a number of these, for example: Buxtehude's *Allemande d'Amour,* Froberger's *Suite in B minor* and *Canzon,* Mattheson's *Fantasy and Minuet* or Muffat's *Fuga Pastorella,* to name a few from many.

Now, may I add a few practical suggestions on basic baroque performance on the piano.

Tempo — Tempo is generally steady in the Baroque, rarely rubato in our sense ("rubato" meant something else in Bach's day). It is rarely indicated (except again by the meticulous French, particularly Couperin). This leaves considerable latitude for personal choice, tempered by the sort of knowledge possessed by every good player in baroque times—that a Sarabande is slow, for example, and a Gigue fast. One should also remember that speed was somewhat limited by the mechanism of the harpsichord which would, for example, have prevented the furious prestos sometimes indulged in the C minor Prelude of "The Well-Tempered Clavier" Volume I.

Legato and Staccato — Bach style and with it the style of Couperin and Scarlatti, must not be thought of as predominantly legato or predominantly non-legato, in spite of ponderous pronouncements in either direction by critics or others. All these composers need a musical employment of both. Couperin characteristically says which he intends. With the others one must guess—or rather decide on the basis of musical evidence. Often several combinations of legato, non-legato, and staccato are permissible. I like Sir Donald Francis Tovey's recommendation that when in doubt as to the internal phrasing of a Bach fugue-subject, for example, the best expedient is to sing it. Almost inevitably a musically logical and convincing phrasing will result—sometimes more than one possibility.

Against a recent trend to treat Bach's music as basically non-legato, one has only to recall one of his own rare statements in which he explains that he wrote the Inventions to initiate the student in the "cantabile manner of playing".

Dynamics — We have offered earlier the opinion that dynamic changes in accordance with the piano's capabilities are permissible and musically valid. These include crescendo, diminuendo, and of course, shading within and at the end of a phrase. One must only reiterate the precautionary advice that none of these resources should be over-used. The continual up-and-down indications of Czerny's and other early editings of Bach's works are clearly a travesty, as would be the style of Bach's own sons with its violent alternations of excessively loud and soft phrases. I suggest that the performer keep the harpsichord and clavichord in mind, but play musically without being unduly restrained by their obvious limitations, the harpsichord's inability to shade, and the clavichord's tiny tone.

Expressiveness — Sentimentality is, of course, completely out of the question, but expressiveness is not. And let it not be supposed that a steady (not rigid) tempo makes expressiveness impossible. The depth of feeling in some of Bach's Sarabandes is unforgettable. Indeed in his Toccatas there are romantic passages in which the freedom of the recitative alternates with the measured expressiveness of the Suites. In general, "we can reject the cowardly evasion of performing baroque music without any passion at all".*

Pedal — Pedal should be used sparingly—sometimes not at all. The harpsichord octave was shorter than the piano's and some difficulties could easily be solved on it that cannot be on the piano. I refer to the problem of sustaining two parts at once in the same hand. Wherever the pedal can be put to good use in connecting notes in a legato line, without blurring other lines, it should be used. None of the later "pedal effects" of Chopin of course, but at the same time none of this didactic "no pedal in Bach" nonsense.

The keyboard music of the Baroque is the source of much of the best music of the era, and it definitely furnishes a most successful approach to the enjoyment of the period. It is also one of the main pillars of a well-rounded pianistic education. The present volume, with its wealth of appealing selections, is an exceptionally fine guide for a pleasurable and instructive journey through the seventeenth and eighteenth centuries.

*Robert Donington, *"The Interpretation of Early Music", p. 22.*

A REVIEW OF BAROQUE ORNAMENTATION

1. Let us start with this one called the *mordent.* It never changes.

   It is performed thus:

   As is the rule with all baroque ornaments, the first note, not the last of the note-group is considered "on the beat", though some necessary evasions are unavoidable in rapid passages where a strict observance of the rule would destroy the rhythm.

2. Now for the source of all evil, the *short trill (shake, praller).*

   It is written and normally played: or

   As you can see, the execution of this ornament starts on the upper neighboring (auxiliary) note. An exception occurs when a legato melodic line approaches the ornament scalewise from above. Then the upper auxiliary note is omitted and we have a three-note ornament starting on the principal note:

   The short trill performed this way is identical with a later (19th century) ornament called the *upper mordent* or *inverted mordent* (also called *snap* or *schneller*).

   In slow tempo the upper neighboring note is sometimes tied to the note it precedes:

   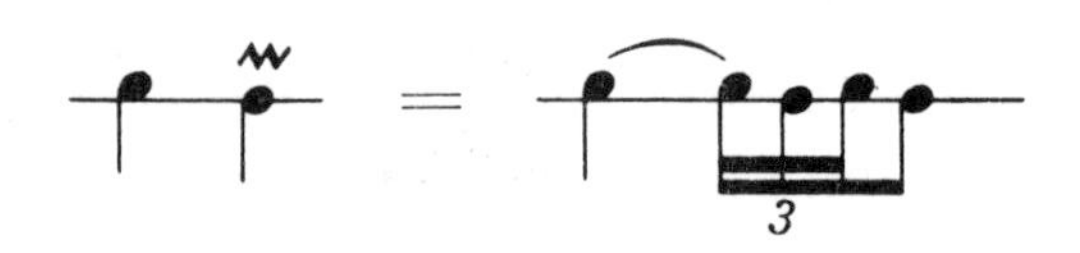

3. The short trill expands into a longer, regular *trill* by the addition of one or more wiggles to the symbol and in performance may be prolonged at will:

   or = etc.

   From here we evolve any number of variants.

   a. A termination is added by a down-stroke:

   = or

b. The beginning of the long trill can be modified by taking once again our basic trill sign and placing before it

a stroke from above:

or a stroke from below:

c. Even more exotic is the combination of beginning and termination:

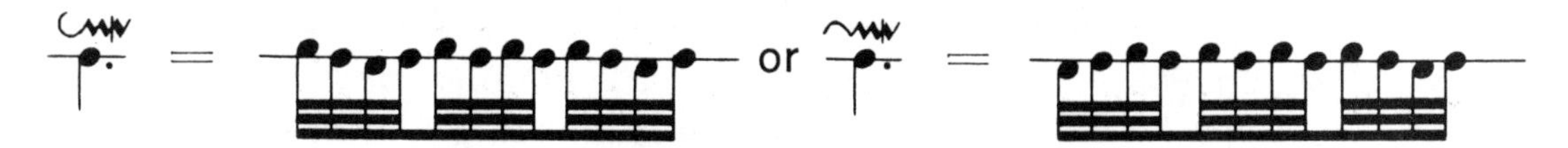

4. The meaning of the sign *tr (trill, trillo)* is often elusive and requires special attention. The sign may indicate a short or a long trill, with or without after-beat, depend- on the period when the music was written, the notation habits of the individual composer, the tempo of the piece, etc. In general the following suggestions may be helpful: in rapid tempo play it as a short trill or as an upper mordent; in slow tempo, or when the sign is over a long note, play it as a long trill with an after-beat.

5. The *turn,* thank heaven, is easy and invariable:

3

If placed between two notes (rare in baroque music):

6. An occasional rarity is the combination which is performed thus:

5

(Relatively less fearsome than it looks; in essence, a short trill with an after-beat.)

7. *Appoggiaturas* are a problem in baroque music mostly because the notation gives no clue as to whether they are "long" ("measured") or "short", somewhat like the 19th century "grace-note", the *acciaccatura.* This edition makes the distinction clear by writing out the long appoggiaturas in conventional notation.

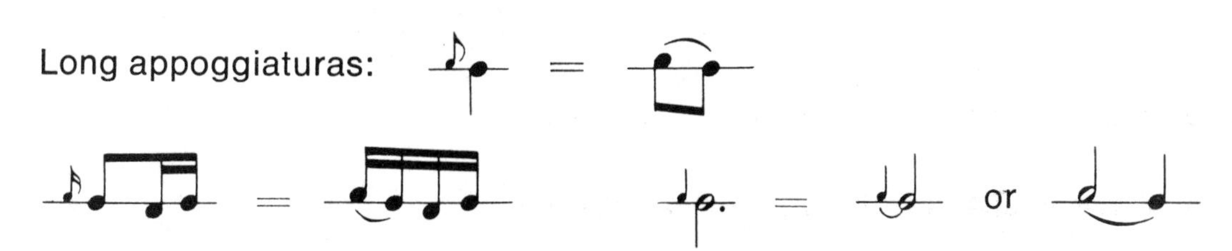

It should be borne in mind that in baroque music even the short appoggiatura is on the beat, and that therefore some slight stress is due the appoggiatura itself, not the note it precedes. This gives a different flavor from that of the later "grace-note".

Short appoggiatura: = "Grace-note":  or =

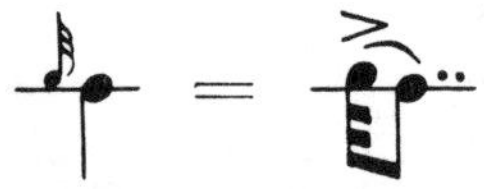

In summing up, the following general rules of baroque ornamentation should be kept in mind:

- ☐ The first note of the note-group is considered "on the beat".
- ☐ Baroque ornaments are diatonic, utilizing only the notes of the scale in which the ornament occurs. Any deviation from this is indicated by an accidental placed under the ornament symbol. (In modulatory passages an accidental is taken for granted.)
- ☐ The longer the note under the ornament sign, the richer the ornament will be.
- ☐ Ornaments should be performed in a manner that does not distort a rhythmic pattern or create false syncopations through undue delay of the final note. In moderate and fast tempos this means playing them quickly; in adagios they are usually more expressive if done deliberately.

One closing word. Rules for performing ornaments are, like everything human, subject to breakdown under stress. One must never sacrifice musical common sense for the sake of a rule. Should a particular ornament prove to be difficult or awkward if performed according to the rules, the player may take certain liberties, which—if done with taste and consistency, would not violate the spirit of baroque performance practices. C. P. E. Bach for example suggests many ways for modifying a short trill under varying tempos.

Intonazione

Pavana

The Earle of Salisbury

William Byrd

Galiardo

Toccata

Jan Pieterszoon Sweelinck

rit.

Bergamasca

Coranto

A Toy

* Varied repetition of the preceding section.

Alman
Moderato
Orlando Gibbons

Aria detto Balletto

Terza Parte
Poco vivo
mf

* Ottava Parte in the original

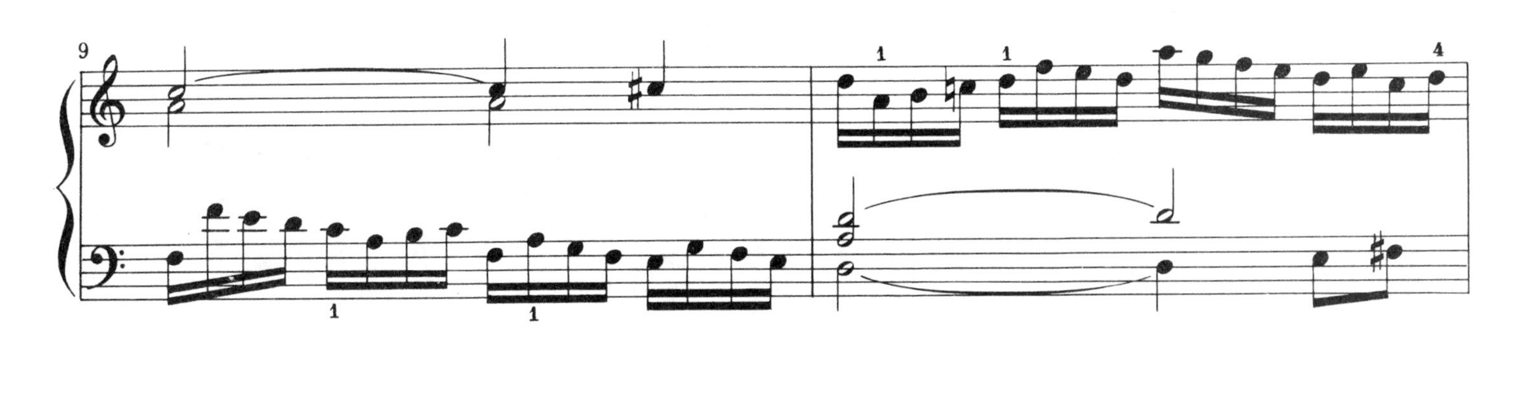

Sarabande

Ricercata

Giovanni Maria Trabacci

Canzon

Suite

Allemande Moderato
Johann Jakob Froberger
mf
Courante Allegretto
mf
mf

Sarabande Larghetto
cresc.
Gigue Allegro
cresc.

Fuga

from "Harmonia Organica" (1645)

Ballet

Allemande d'Amour

from Suite No. 6

Variations on an Aria by Lully

(Rofilis)

Dietrich Buxtehude

Variation 2

Double

L.H.
Variation 3 Con moto

Prelude

Courante

John Blow

Rigadoon

A New Irish Tune

Ground

9
11
5
2
mf
13
p
15
17
3
2
f

19
21
p
23
25
mf
27

p
f
p
cresc.

Suite No. 4

Henry Purcell

Courante Con moto

13
18
23
Saraband
Andante
6
12

Victory Dance and Festival

from Biblical Sonata No. 1 "The Battle Between David and Goliath"

Johann Kuhnau

33
cresc.
40
Gavotte
Johann Kuhnau
Andante con moto
5
9
13

Song of the Bridesmaids

from Biblical Sonata No. 3 "Jacob's Wedding"

Fantasie

19
22
25
28
p
30
32
mf
mf

35
Fugue
Johann Pachelbel
Allegretto
mf
4
7
10
tr

Fantasie and Menuett

from Suite No. 5

Adagio
segue
Menuett Allegretto
cresc.
cresc.

Chaconne

from "Melpomene" Suite

Johann Kaspar Ferdinand Fischer

mf
f
espr.

Passepied

from "Melpomene" Suite

Johann Kaspar Ferdinand Fischer

Prelude and Fugue

from "Ariadne Musica"

Allegro moderato

Johann Caspar Ferdinand Fischer

Allegretto
mp
fr
mf
f

Gavotte and Bourrée

Menuet

Gigue

où il y a un Canon

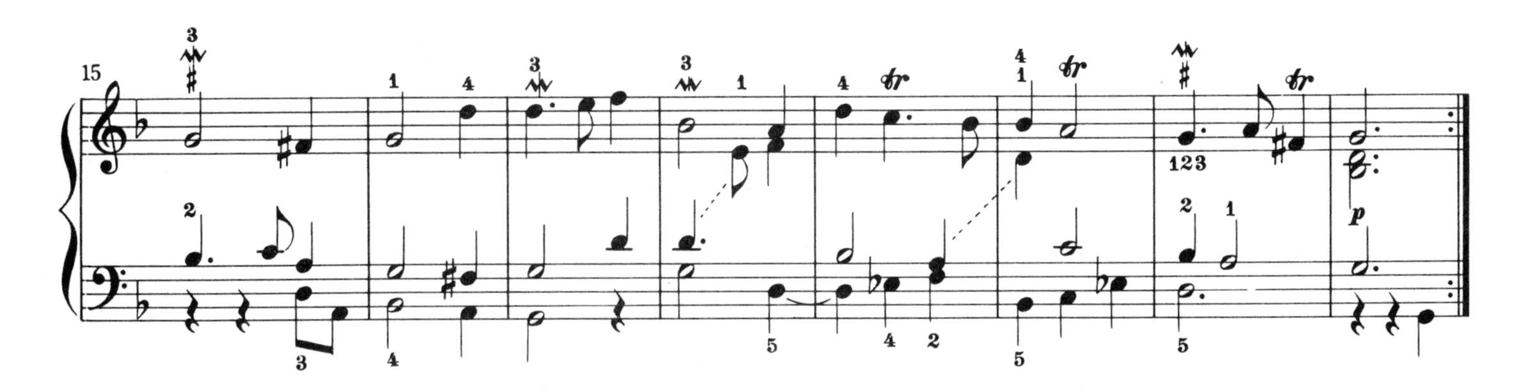

Air Encien

Gavotte

Les Grâces Naturèles

Natural Charm - Suite de la Bontems

1

François Couperin

2

L' Âme-en-Peine

Anguished Soul

Le Réveille - Matin

The Alarm Clock

François Couperin

mf
p
cresc.
f
p
cresc.
f

24
26
28
cresc.
30
32
34

Le Rossignol-en-Amour

Nightingale in Love

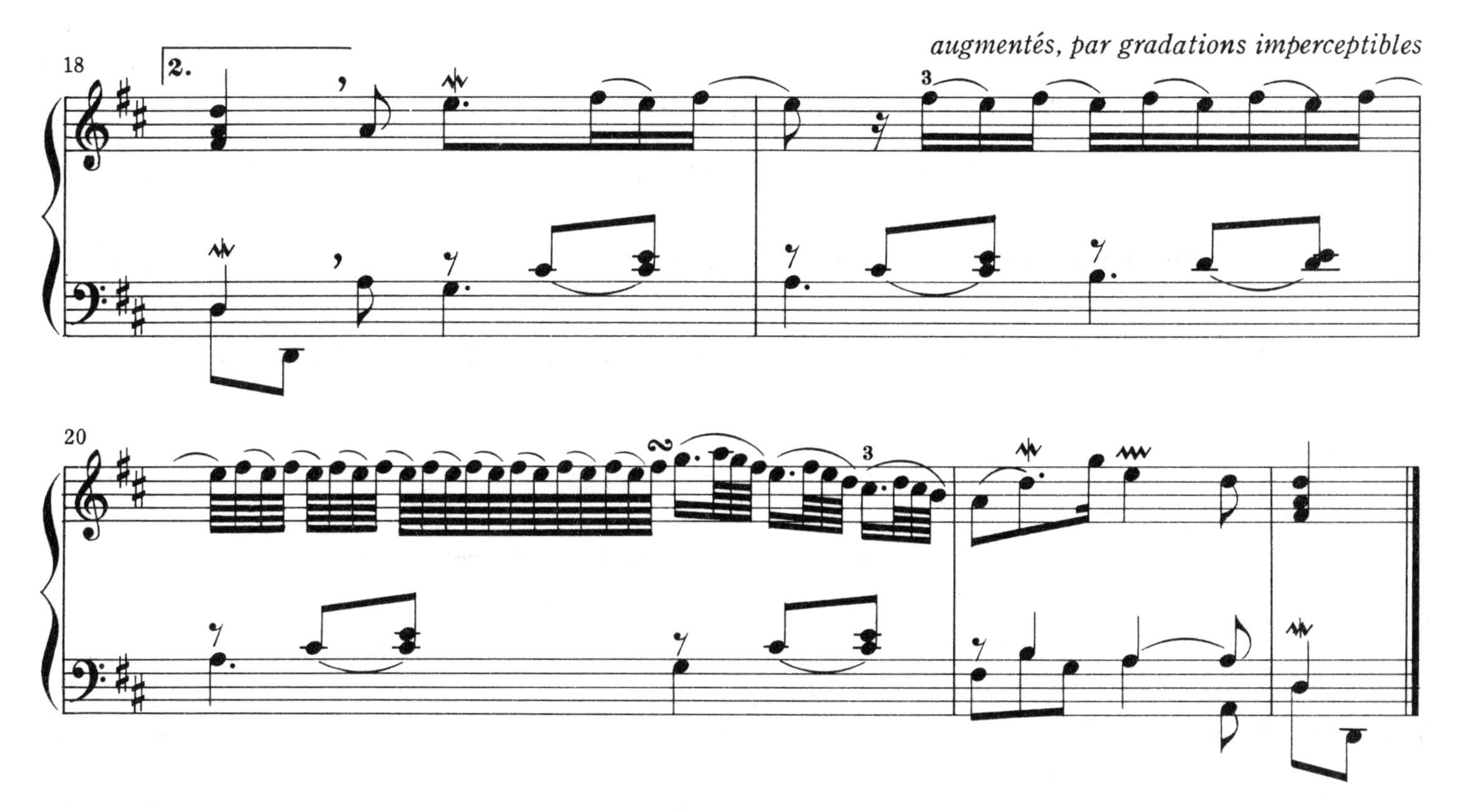

Fanfarinette

Little Brass Band

Allegretto

Jean Philippe Rameau

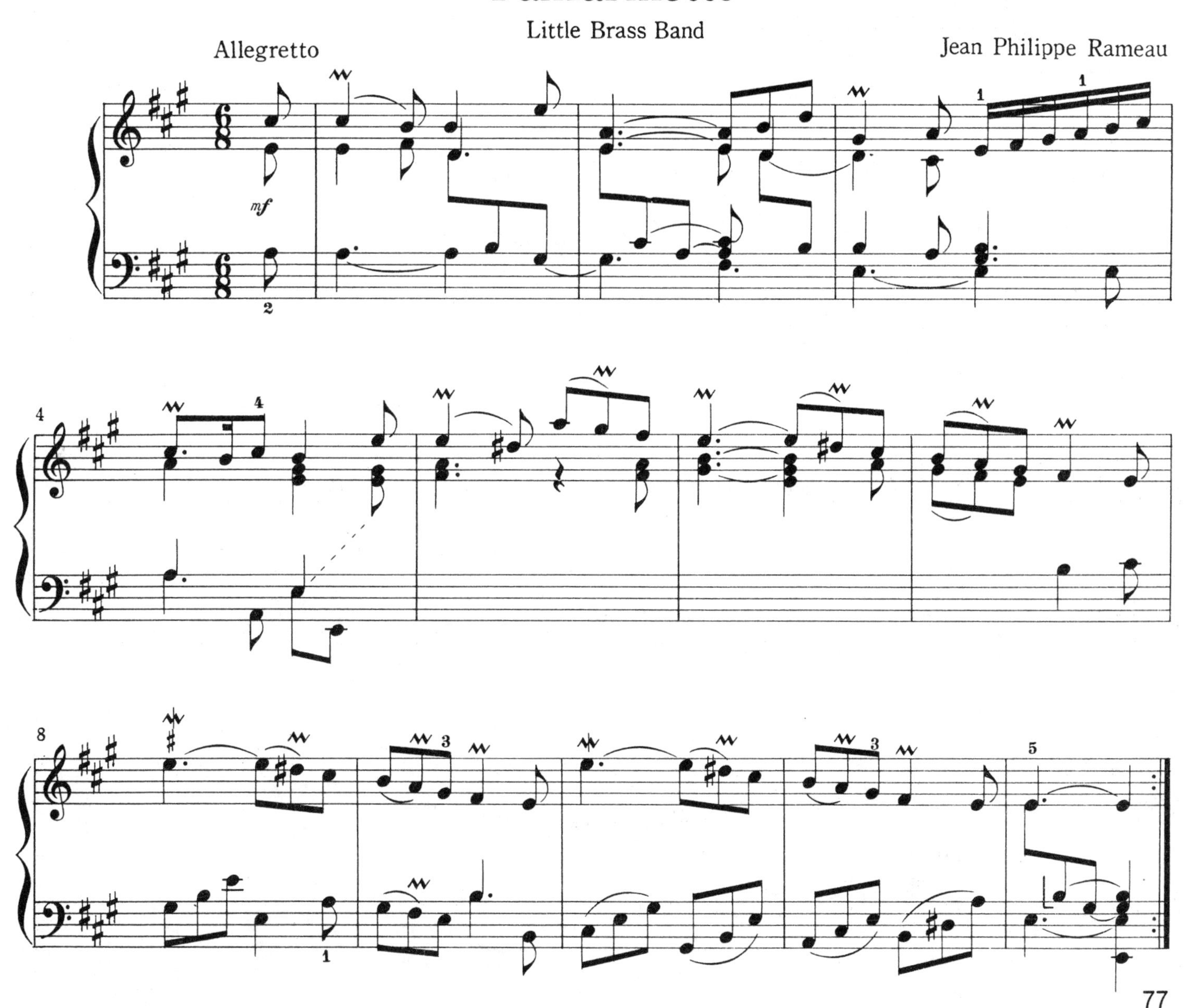

13
p
mf
18
f
23
cresc.
29
p
34
cresc.
f
39

La Villageoise

Village Girl – Rondeau

Jean Philippe Rameau

dim.

Two Sarabandes

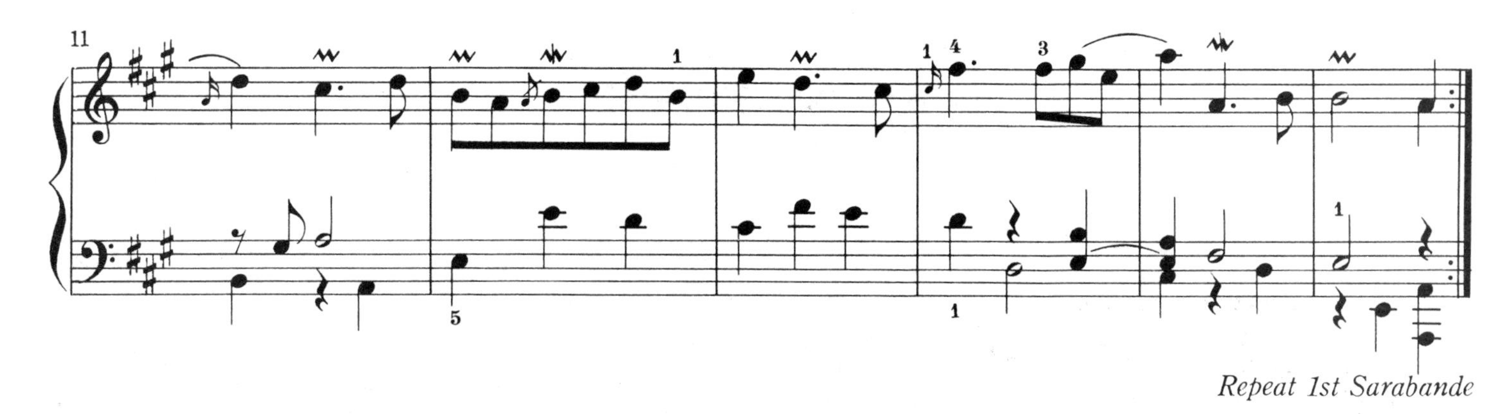

Repeat 1st Sarabande

La Boiteuse

Lame Girl

La Gemissante

Moaning Girl - Rondeau

Jean François Dandrieu

2nd Couplet
D.C. al Fine

Le Caquet

Cackle

Jean François Dandrieu

mf
p

La Joyeuse

 * Play Rondeau - First Couplet - Rondeau - Second Couplet - Rondeau.

2nd Couplet
D.C. al
D. C. al Fine
p
mp

Passacaglia

Christian Friedrich Witt*

* At one time this work was attributed to J.S. Bach.

p
mp
cresc.
f

76
79
82
85
88
92
f
p
(tr)

Two Choral Preludes

on "Fröhlich Soll Mein Herze Springen"

1

Johann Gottfried Walther

2

Little Prelude No. 6

Inventio No. 13
Two-Voice Invention
Johann Sebastian Bach
Moderato
mf
f
dim.

f
dim.
p
cresc.
f

Inventio No. 14

Two-Voice Invention

Inventio No. 3

Two-Voice Invention

Johann Sebastian Bach

30
cresc.
35
f
tr
mf
40
f
45
p
50
mf
tr
55
tr

Scherzo

from Partita No. 3

Johann Sebastian Bach

Sinfonia No. 15

Three-Voice Invention

cresc.
f
p
mf
cresc.
f
mf

Fugue in C Major

Johann Sebastian Bach

Fantasie

Johann Sebastian Bach

cresc.

mp
R.H.
pp
cresc.

31
mf
33
cresc.
f
35
37
mf
39
cresc.
f

Praeludium XI

from "The Well-Tempered Clavier," Book 1

Johann Sebastian Bach

Fuga XI

from "The Well-Tempered Clavier," Book 1

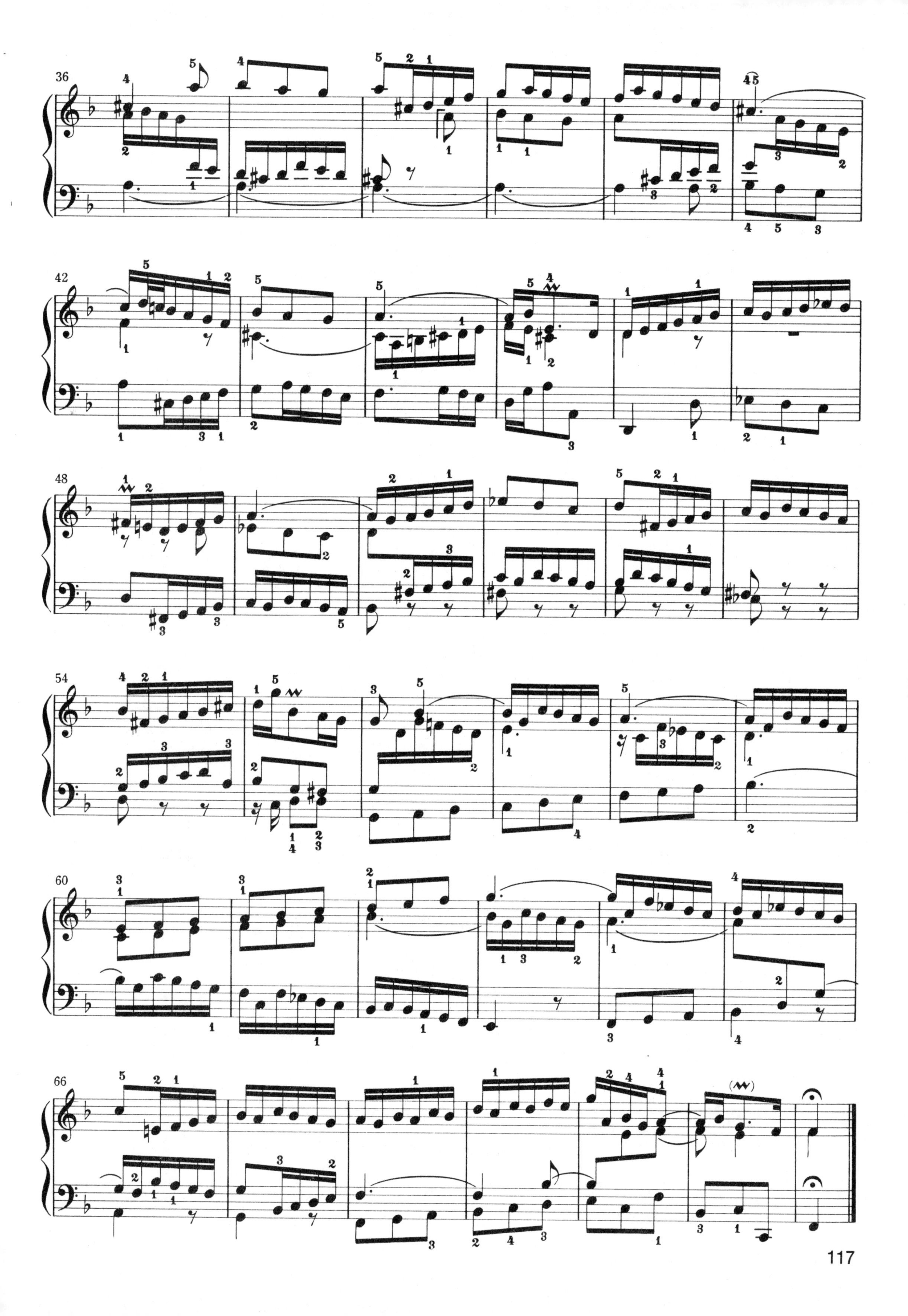

Praeludium VII

from "The Well-Tempered Clavier," Book 2

* in the autograph ** in the autograph

Fuga VII

a 4 Voci from "The Well-Tempered Clavier," Book 2

Allegro moderato

French Suite No. 6

Courante Allegro con brio
L.H.

L. H.

Sarabande Andante sostenuto
mf espr.

Gavotte Allegretto
mf
mf
cresc.
p
cresc.
f

Polonaise Andante con moto
p
mp
p
cresc.
mf
dim.

 * Quarter notes may be played staccato.

20
24
28
32
35
39

Menuet Moderato
Gigue Vivace

Fantasia

George Frideric Handel

21
mf
f
25
p
28
cresc.
f
31
p
34
cresc.
f

Sonatina

George Frideric Handel

mf
f
dim.
p
cresc.
f
p
mf
p

25
mf
f
28
p
f
31
p
34
f
37
40
p cresc.
f

Air and Variations

"The Harmonious Blacksmith" from Suite No. 5

Var. 2
Var. 3

Var. 4

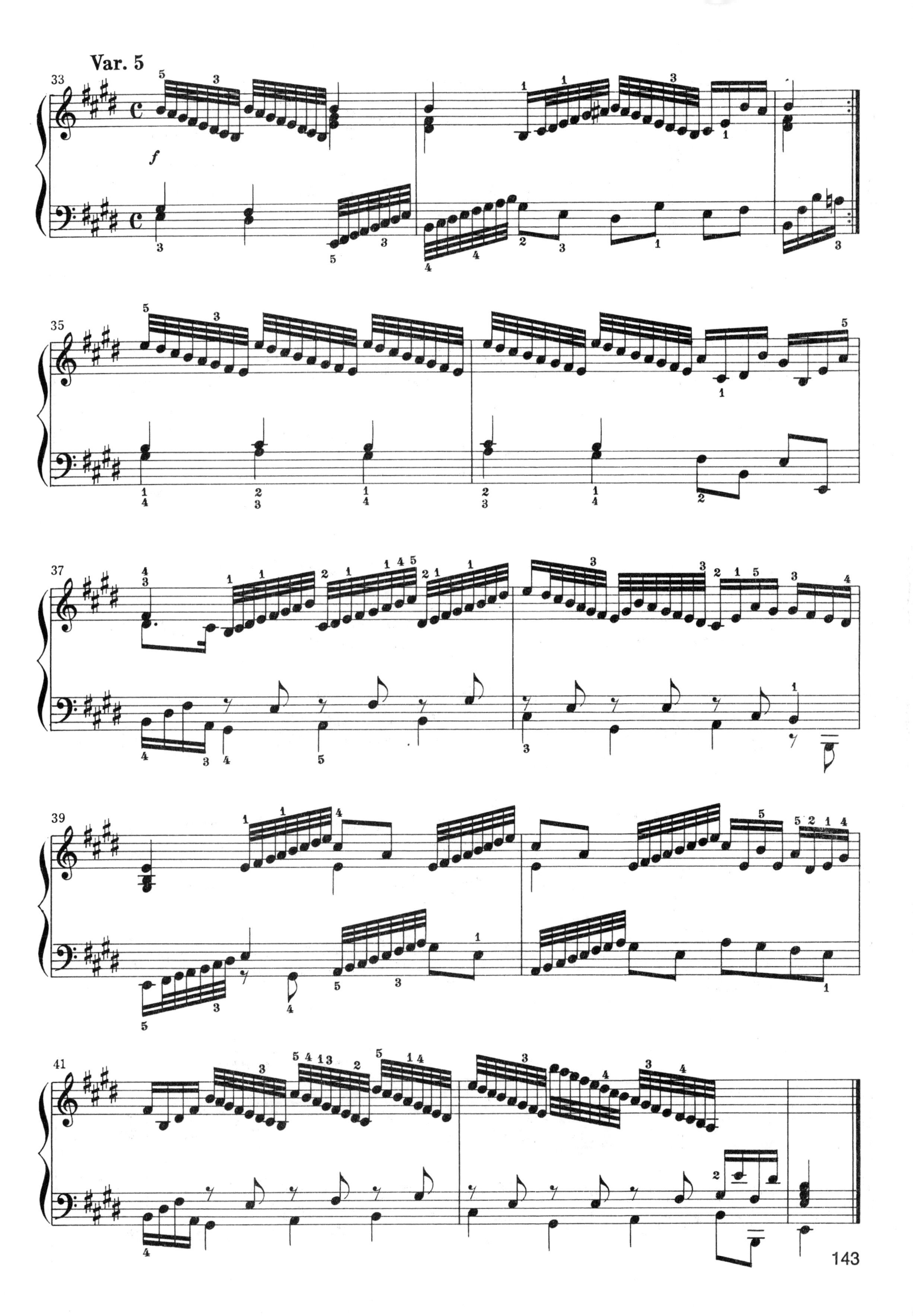
Var. 5
f

Suite No. 11

Courante Allegretto
mf

cresc.
cresc.

Sarabande Larghetto
cresc.
Var. 1
cresc.
dim.
cresc.

Var. 2
cresc.
Gigue Allegro

Bourrée

Loure

Georg Philipp Telemann

Rigaudon

Cantabile and Fugue

13
19
25
31
37
43

Fantasia

B minor

Georg Philipp Telemann

Con pompa
1 Repeat Allegro

Andante Maestoso

from Sonata in B♭ major

Benedetto Marcello

Four Arias

1

Bernardo Pasquini

3
Moderato
4
Allegro

Sarabanda and Giga

from Suite in G minor

Domenico Zipoli

cresc.
f
p
cresc.
f
p
mf
f
p
mf
f
p
f

Theme and Variations

from Partita in A minor

Domenico Zipoli

Var. 3 Animato
Var. 4
p
cresc.
mf
dim.
f

Var. 5
mp
cresc.
p
cresc.
f
Var. 6 Allegro
mf
cresc.
mf
cresc.

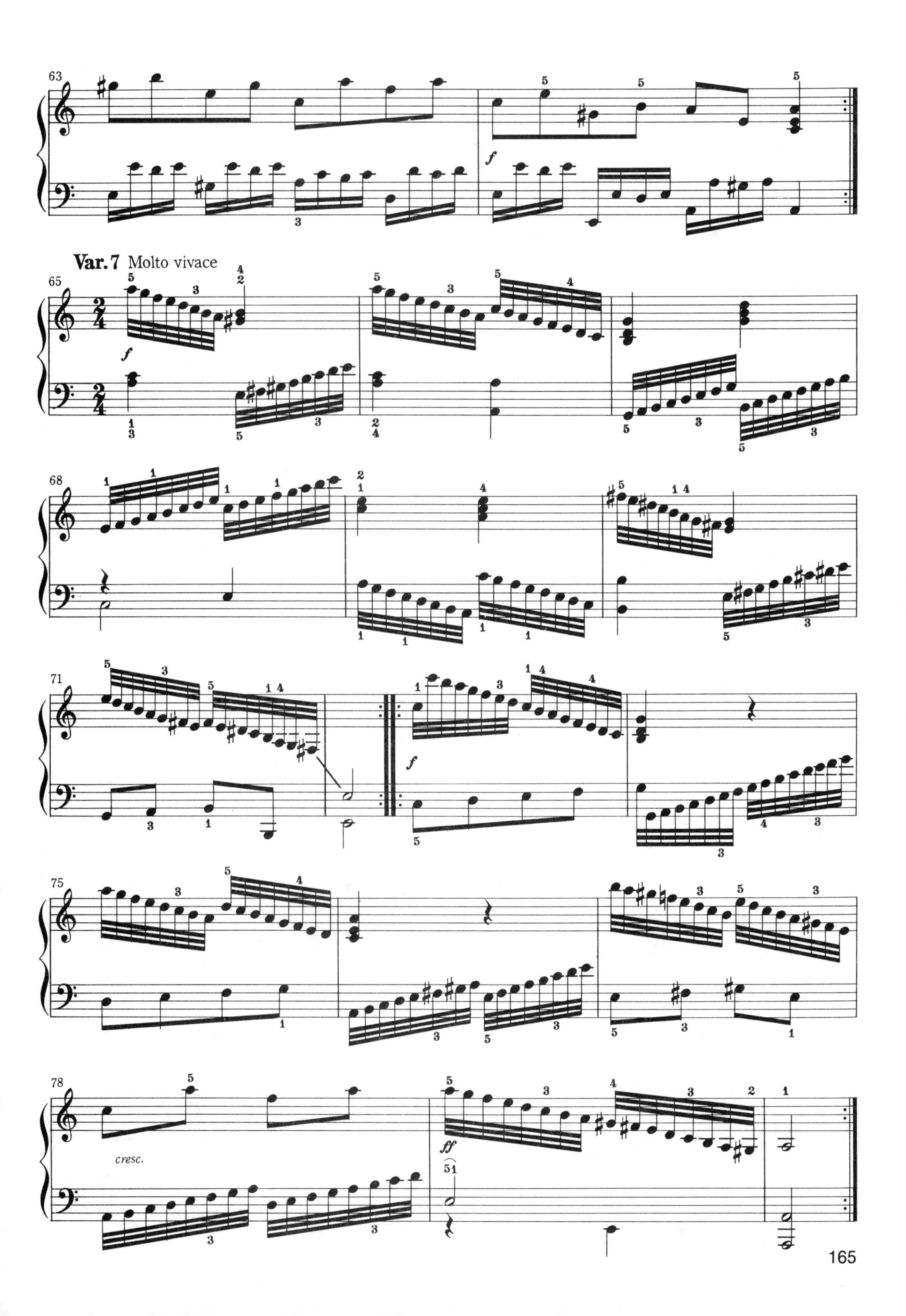
Var. 7 Molto vivace
cresc.

Two Divertimenti

1

Francesco Durante

allarg.
R.H.
2
Allegro
cresc.
cresc.
cresc.

Toccata

Leonardo Leo

34
mf
39
p
mf
p cresc.
44
f
f
50
p
56
cresc.
f
61
p cresc.
f

Sonata

L. 388

Domenico Scarlatti

cresc.

Sonata

L. 497

Domenico Scarlatti

23
26
30
34
38
tr

Sonata

L. 263

30
36
42
48
mf
cresc.
53
59

64
69
74
79
84

Hornpipe

Allegro energico
Jean Baptiste Loeillet
f
p
f
mf
f
dim.
p
mf
cresc.
f

Siciliana

Fuga Pastorella

Gottlieb Muffat

Toccata and Fugue

Fuga Allegretto
rit.

Two Pieces

from "Musical Pastime at the Clavier"

1

2

Villanella

from a Sonata in F major

cresc.
f
mp
f

Air en Gavotte

Christoph Graupner

Sonata

tr
p
cresc.
poco
a
poco
f a piacere
poco meno mosso
p
mp
f
mp
f

rit.
a tempo

Adagio

from Sonata in G minor

Giovanni Battista Martini

34
39
cresc.
45
f
50
p
cresc.
p
cresc.
55
f
dim.
p
61

Presto (Toccata)

from Sonata in D major

Pietro Domenico Paradisi

f
p
f > p
mp
mf
cresc.
f
rit.

Toccata

Carlos Seixas

p cresc.

Sonata

No. 84

Antonio Soler

36
cresc.
42
più f
49
1.
2.
55
mp
60
cresc.
65
dim. sempre

p
cresc.
f
p
cresc.
f
f
p
cresc.
f
f
più f

Praeambulum

22
mf
25
31
34
37
p
cresc.

cresc.

Clavier Partie

Gigue Allegro
mp
f
p
cresc.
1.
2.

La Tendre

Andante sostenuto
Christoph Nichelmann
p
cresc.
1.
2.
cresc.
mf
pp
mf
pp
poco rit.
a tempo
mf

La Gaillarde

p
cresc.
mf
p
mf
f

Buffone

Polonaise

Wilhelm Friedemann Bach

17
p
cresc.
mf
20
cresc.
f
dim.
p cresc.
24
mf
28
p
32
cresc.
cresc.
36
f
1.
2.

Capriccio

Carl Philipp Emanuel Bach

stacc.
stacc.

Sonata

Carl Philipp Emanuel Bach

39
p
f
46
53
ff
p
f
60
p
cresc.
66
1.
f
69
2.
p
rit.

Allegretto
mf
p
f
cresc.
poco a poco

Presto di molto

Adagio

from Sonata in D major

Baldassare Galuppi

p *mp* *cresc.* *p* *mp* *cresc.* *mf*

Les Carillons

Johann Philipp Kirnberger

Alternativo
p
cresc.
mp
cresc.
mf
p
D. C. Majore

Sonata

Johann Philipp Kirnberger

cresc.

51
54
tr
57
61
64
f
68
p

mf
f
mp
f
p
cresc.
f

EDITORIAL NOTES

Page

21 Intonazione (Gabrieli) Note values were cut in half to avoid the now seldom used *breve* 𝅜

24 Toccata (Sweelinck) This work has the subtitle *Fantasia Quarti Toni,* meaning *Fantasia in the Fourth Mode.* "Fourth Mode" is another name for the hypo-phrygian scale.

27 Bergamasca (Scheidt) The first eight variations of an extended work.

30 Aria detto Balletto (Frescobaldi) Some variations omitted.

35 Canzon (Froberger) This is the first section of a three-part work.

68 Minuet (Lully) Written for King Louis XIV, this is believed to be the earliest Minuet in the instrumental literature.

70 Les Grâces Naturèles (Couperin) The slurs in this piece are the editor's; they are replacing Couperin's slanting strokes which he placed between certain notes to indicate the joining of these notes into a (legato) group.

76 Le Rossignol-en-Amour (Couperin) See page 70 (Les Grâces Naturèles)

90 Passacaglia (Witt) For a long time this piece was believed to be the work of J. S. Bach. Some variations omitted.

102 Inventio No. 3 (J. S. Bach) Our copy is based on a facsimile edition of Bach's original autograph. This is one of the few Bach keyboard works which contain the master's original articulation marks. Unfortunately, Bach's placement of his slurs is very often rather vague; it is hard to determine over which note a slur begins and where it ends. Our interpretation of these marks, arrived at after careful analysis of the work's motivic structure, is, we believe, a logical reconstruction of the composer's probable intention and should facilitate a smooth rendition of the piece.

157 Andante Maestoso (Marcello) The Editor's title.

162 Theme and Variations (Zipoli) Some variations omitted.

BIOGRAPHICAL SKETCHES OF COMPOSERS

d'Anglebert, Jean Henri, b. 1635, Paris—d. 1691, Paris. A pupil of Chambonnières and important predecessor of Couperin. His clavecin music rivals that of his eminent contemporaries and forms an important step in the development of French keyboard style.

Bach, Carl Philipp Emanuel, b. 1714, Weimar, Germany—d. 1788, Hamburg. Second son of J. S. Bach and, from an historic and stylistic point of view, the most significant one. Widely acclaimed throughout Europe, he was for many years leading court musician of Frederick the Great in Berlin. His major medium of expression was the keyboard, whose literature he enriched with works of great originality, dramatic power, and an almost "romantic" expressiveness. Had a fundamental role in the development of the sonata form and exerted considerable influence on the great triumvirate of Classicism: Haydn, Mozart, and Beethoven. His "Essay on the True Art of Clavier Playing" is not only one of the first important piano methods, but also a definitive source on the style and performance practices of his time.

Bach, Johann Sebastian, b. 1685, Eisenach, Germany—d. 1750, Leipzig. Towering member of the family that played a leading role in German music for over one hundred and fifty years, one of the greatest musical minds of all ages. During his lifetime he was famous as composer and as performer on the organ, although his entire sphere of musical activity was confined to a relatively small geographical area. Married twice and had twenty children. Composed a profusion of masterpieces, oratorios, cantatas, masses, concerti and a large number of keyboard works which represent the summit of baroque composition.

Bach, Wilhelm Friedemann, b. 1710, Weimar, Germany—d. 1784, Berlin. Eldest son of J. S. Bach and considered by many the most talented. Possibly the greatest performer on the organ in Germany after the death of his father. A malicious distortion of history has presented his life, actually one of musical devotion and sobriety but embittered by frustration, as the tragedy of an alcoholic genius. His music reflects the conflict between the intellectuality of the high baroque and the emotionalism of the transition toward classicism.

Blow, John, b. 1649, Newark, England—d. 1708, London. Organist at the court, at Westminster Abbey, at St. Paul's Cathedral. Prolific, dignified composer of important church and harpsichord music. Scarcely less renowned than his pupil, Henry Purcell.

Buxtehude, Dietrich, b. 1637, Helsingor, Denmark (now in Sweden)—d. 1707, Lübeck, Germany. Towering figure among composers and organists of his time. His fugues and choral preludes, full of rich polyphony, dramatic power and often conceived in a grandiose design, had great influence on Bach, who, at one time, walked two hundred miles to meet him and hear him play. (Later Bach declined the opportunity to become his successor as organist in Lübeck because the post required that he marry Buxtehude's daughter.)

Byrd, William, b. 1542, Lincolnshire—d. 1623, Stondon, Essex. Dominant figure among the first generation of English composers of the Elizabethan period.

Chambonnières, Jacques Champion de, b. 1602 (place unknown)—d. 1672, Paris. Leading court musician of Louis XIII and Louis XIV, most celebrated harpsichordist of his day. Founder of the French school of keyboard composition. Introduced the Couperin family to the king, with far-reaching results for French music.

Couperin, François, b. 1668, Paris—d. 1733, Paris. Known as "le Grand" during his lifetime; one of the most eminent figures in French music. A lifelong friend of kings (Louis XIV and Louis XV), teacher of princes, harpsichordist, organist and theorist. His suites ("ordres"), consisting of finely chiseled, sometimes deeply expressive, often programmatic or witty dance and character pieces, are shining gems of baroque keyboard literature and exerted considerable influence on numerous successive generations of masters from Bach to Debussy. The first keyboard instrumentalist to use his thumb in systematic fingering; also wrote an important treatise on performance, "L'Art de toucher le Clavecin".

Dandrieu, Jean Francois, b. 1682, Paris—d. 1738, Paris. Organist, harpsichordist, composer; notable contemporary of Couperin and Rameau. His three volumes of pieces for the clavecin represent an important part of French instrumental literature.

Daquin, Louis Claude, b. 1694, Paris—d. 1772, Paris. Appeared before Louis XIV at the age of six as a prodigy on the harpsichord. Succeeded Dandrieu as organist of the royal chapel. Wrote many charming pieces for the harpsichord.

Durante, Francesco, b. 1684, Naples—d. 1755, Naples. Teacher of an entire generation of eminent Italian composers, including Pergolesi. Was a very popular composer of his day, although only a few of his compositions were published during his lifetime. In his music rigid baroque traditions are mellowed by Neapolitan belcanto flavors.

Fischer, Johann Kaspar Ferdinand, b. 1665 (place unknown)—d. 1746, Rastatt, Germany. Noted conductor and composer of considerable influence on Bach. His very melodic, finely formed suites for clavier follow a French pattern in their sequences, with interpolations of Minuets, Passepieds, etc. His *Ariadne Musica,* a collection of twenty Preludes and Fugues—each in a different major and minor key—is a direct predecessor of *The Well-Tempered Clavier.*

Frescobaldi, Girolamo, b. 1583, Farrara—d. 1643, Rome. Greatest Italian composer of the early Baroque; world famous as the organist at St. Peter's in Rome, where thousands flocked to listen to him. His works, with their expressive power and imaginative technical mystery, opened new paths for the instrumental literature of his time.

Froberger, Johann Jakob, b. 1616, Stuttgart, Germany—d. 1667, Hericourt, France. Pupil of Frescobaldi, court organist in Vienna, famous throughout Europe as composer and organ virtuoso. As a pioneer in establishing the four-movement plan of the keyboard suite (Allemande-Courante-Sarabande-Gigue) he was of great influence on Bach.

Gabrieli, Giovanni, b. 1557, Venice—d. 1612, Venice. Came from a family of distinguished musicians. Studied with his uncle Andrea Gabrieli, as did Sweelinck, mentioned below. Was chief organist at St. Mark's in Venice. Acclaimed internationally as teacher and bold innovator in all fields of composition: choral, orchestral, instrumental.

Galuppi, Baldassare, b. 1706, Venice—d. 1785, Venice. Celebrated composer of many comic operas—112 in all—vice *maestro di capella* at St. Mark's and director of the Conservatory in Venice. Folk elements of his native city are clearly discernible in his music. His keyboard sonatas represent an important transitional stage in the development of the form, between the late Baroque and the early classics.

Gibbons, Orlando, b. 1583, Oxford—d. 1625, Canterbury. Outstanding composer of the later group of English virginalists. Their technique and writing style for the keyboard, advanced beyond anything found elsewhere in Europe, had great influence on future harpsichord, and even piano music.

Graupner, Christoph, b. 1683, Kirchberg, Saxony —d. 1760, Darmstadt. Notable contemporary of Bach and Handel, a pupil of Kuhnau. Was regarded as the outstanding musician of Germany in his day and was invited to succeed Kuhnau as cantor of the St. Thomas Church in Leipzig; only after he failed to assume the post was the position offered to J. S. Bach.

Handel, George Frideric, b. 1685, Halle, Germany —d. 1759, London. With Bach, the greatest name in baroque music. A cosmopolitan master whose international fame, success, and influence, especially in the field of opera and oratorio, were unsurpassed in his time. His music for the harpsichord is of relatively minor importance but high in quality. His later years in London made him the virtual dictator of English music. The blending of German, Italian, and French influences resulted in a style rarely equalled for sheer vitality and expressiveness. "He is the master of us all"—proclaimed Haydn.

Hurlebusch, Conrad, b. 1696, Braunschweig, Germany—d. 1765, Amsterdam. Court conductor in Stockholm, later organist in Hamburg and Amsterdam. Widely respected and popular composer of operas, various instrumental works and a great many songs ("odes"), eleven of which Leopold Mozart included in his "Little Note-book for Wolfgang".

Kindermann, Johann Erasmus, b. 1616, Nuremberg—d. 1655, Nuremberg. Respected as organist and composer in various media, instrumental and vocal. Particularly interesting are his smaller keyboard pieces, light, melodiously chromatic and almost popular in character—a rather rare phenomenon in the instrumental literature of the early Baroque.

Kirnberger, Johann Philipp, b. 1721, Saalfeld, Germany—d. 1783, Berlin. Pupil of J. S. Bach, notable composer of the Berlin School, and leading, although somewhat controversial, theorist of his time. A transitional composer, strongly influenced by C. P. E. Bach, with perhaps a bit more rococo lightness and an affinity for finely formed melodic miniatures. His clavier sonatas stand at the threshold of Haydn's early Classicism.

Krebs, Johann Ludwig, b. 1713, Buttelstadt, Germany—d. 1780, Altenburg. Organist and composer, pupil of J. S. Bach at the St. Thomas School in Leipzig. Held several important organ posts, performed brilliantly on both organ and harpsichord. A highly skilled, esteemed composer whose style lies somewhere between the conservative baroque and the "gallant" traditions.

Krieger, Johann, b. 1651, Nuremberg—d. 1735, Zittau. Court organist at Bayreuth. Only a few of his works were published during his lifetime, but they were well known and respected. His keyboard pieces elicited admiring remarks from Handel.

Kuhnau, Johann, b. 1660, Geising, Saxony—d. 1732, Leipzig. Organist at the St. Thomas Church in Leipzig before Bach. Very influential as composer and writer on music. The first to write piano sonatas in several movements; composed some of the earliest "program music" for the keyboard in his "biblical sonatas", in which every section depicts a different scene from the Scriptures.

Leo, Leonardo, b. 1694, Brindisi, Italy—d. 1744, Naples. Lived and worked in Naples throughout his life as organist at the Royal Chapel and teacher at the Conservatory. An outstanding composer of high-baroque traditions, with native Italian overtones. He wrote many works of enduring beauty for the church, for the stage, and for various instruments, including the harpsichord.

Loeillet, Jean Baptiste, b. 1680, Ghent, Belgium —d. 1730, London. Renowned flutist and composer, from 1705 a popular figure in London musical circles. His works, well-constructed and melodic, present a lighter, rather homophonic side of baroque keyboard music.

Lully, Jean Baptiste, b. 1632, Florence, Italy—d. 1687, Paris. Moved to France at the age of fourteen and had a spectacular career. Under the patronage of Louis XIV he became the leading musical figure of his adopted country, with immense influence on composition in all fields. Introduced the minuet as part of ballet scenes in his operas.

Maichelbeck, Franz Anton, b. 1702, Reichenau, Germany—d. 1750, Freiburg. German composer whose long stay in Italy as a student influenced his keyboard music toward the Italian homophonic style. His clavier sonatas—actually suites consisting of dance and character pieces—adhere in style to late Baroque and "gallant" traditions.

Mattheson, Johann, b. 1681, Hamburg—d. 1764, Hamburg. One of the most interesting and versatile personalities of the Baroque; a close friend of Handel. He was not only an important composer, conductor, and pioneer writer on musical subjects, but also a historian, jurist, theologian, diplomat, and acclaimed singer of tenor parts at the Hamburg opera.

Marcello, Benedetto, b. 1686, Venice—d. 1739, Brescia. Venetian nobleman, highly cultured, immensely talented composer. His main opus is a monumental collection of Psalms for voices and continuo, but he wrote works of great beauty in many other media.

Martini, Giovanni Battista, b. 1706, Bologna—d. 1784, Bologna. "Padre Martini", Italian composer, theorist and teacher of immense erudition and international fame. Friend of kings and princes, his generosity was legendary, as in his recognizing the promise of the boy Mozart and doing all he could to further his career. Wrote learned books on music history and theory, and composed much excellent music of lasting value and appeal.

Muffat, Gottlieb, b. 1690, Passau, Austria—d. 1770, Vienna. Important German composer of Scottish descent. Spent most of his life in Vienna as court organist and musical tutor of the royal family. Rich melodic invention characterizes his works which form an interesting link between keyboard styles of the French and German Baroque. His father, George, was a composer of equal repute and of considerable historical importance.

Nichelmann, Christoph, b. 1717, Treuenbrietzen, Germany—d. 1783, Hamburg. German harpsichordist and writer on music. A pupil of J. S. Bach in Leipzig, later studied with Quantz in Berlin where he was appointed to the court to accompany the flute playing of Frederick the Great. His clavier music, which can best be described as German rococo, was highly esteemed by his contemporaries.

Pachelbel, Johann, b. 1653, Nuremberg—d. 1706, Nuremberg. Outstanding figure among the pre-Bach generation of German organist-composers. Bach was strongly influenced by his works, particularly toward the development of the choral prelude.

Paradisi, Pietro Domenico, b. 1707, Naples—d. 1791, Venice. Italian composer and pedagogue. Settled in London in 1746 and lived there for many years before returning to Italy. His sonatas, highly regarded by Clementi and Cramer, represent an important segment of eighteenth century Italian keyboard literature and are of lasting appeal.

Pasquini, Bernardo, b. 1630, Florence—d. 1710, Rome. Outstanding master of the Italian Baroque; brilliant organist and composer of great originality and versatility; renowned teacher of Durante, Muffat and others. The first Italian composer of keyboard suites.

Pergolesi, Giovanni, b. 1710, Ancona, Italy—d. 1736, Pozzuoli. Leading master of a "gallant", popularly-oriented branch of the Neapolitan School. In spite of his early death at the age of twenty-six, he exercised important influence in several directions: his enormously successful comic opera, *La Serva Padrona,* became the model of eighteenth century Italian opera buffa; his solo and trio-sonatas foreshadow numerous elements of the mature classic sonata ("singing allegro", contrasting second theme, etc.). After his untimely death, to capitalize on his spectacular career, many works not his were ascribed to him.

Purcell, Henry, b. 1659, London—d. 1695, London. Most eminent member of a famous musical family. Last of the great English composers of the Baroque. Had immensely successful career as organist, composer. Particularly significant was his music for numerous plays, and his opera *Dido and Aeneas,* written for an English girls' school. His keyboard works, with their dramatic intensity and expressive lyricism, are unique in the harpsichord literature of his time.

Rameau, Jean Philippe, b. 1683, Dijon, France—d. 1764, Paris. One of the most original and influential among French composers of the eighteenth century; acclaimed by many as the greatest French musician of all time. Devoted most of his creative energies to composing for the stage. His operas broke new paths with their dramatic power, rich harmonies and inventive orchestral coloring. His clavecin music, in contrast to Couperin's ethereal clarity, is fuller, more down-to-earth, but none-the-less masterly. His revolutionary treatise on harmony established the theoretical principles of this subject, still pertinent today.

Rathgeber, Valentin, b. 1682 (Germany)—d. 1750. German monk, composer of numerous works for the church. His reputation, however, is preserved more by a few light-hearted works, decidedly secular in spirit, such as his "Musical Pastime at the Clavier", a collection of charming keyboard miniatures.

Scarlatti, Domenico, b. 1685, Naples—d. 1757, Madrid. Son of Alessandro Scarlatti, whose eminence dominated Domenico's early years. His entire life changed when he was appointed Master of the Royal Chapel in Lisbon. After one visit to Naples in 1724 he returned to Lisbon and later, for the rest of his life, to Spain, where his pupil, the Princess Maria Barbara of Portugal, had married the crown prince and soon became queen of Spain. Scarlatti's music shows a complete identification with his adopted country. Lacking almost entirely in Italian characteristics, it reflects the richness and vitality of the Spanish folk idiom, and in its originality of keyboard treatment shows considerable awareness of guitar techniques. Scarlatti was much ahead of his age in keyboard writing; his music is one of the sources of modern piano technique.

Scheidt, Samuel, b. 1587, Halle, Germany—d. 1654, Halle. Outstanding instrumental composer of 17th century Germany. Especially important is his contribution to the development of the art of organ-variations.

Seixas, Carlos, b. 1704, Coimbra, Portugal—d. 1742, Lisbon. One of the best of the harpsichord composers influenced by Domenico Scarlatti, whom he knew during Scarlatti's presence at the court of King John of Portugal. Developed a very individual style of harpsichord writing, highly personal but quite Portuguese in its affinity for folk music.

Soler, Antonio, b. 1729, Olot, Catalonia, Spain—d. 1783, Escorial Monastery. Most noted pupil of Domenico Scarlatti, whose audacious keyboard style received further elaboration in Soler's sonatas, which are even more Spanish in character than Scarlatti's. A lifetime spent in monasteries evidently detracted nothing from the joyous vitality of Soler's music, which is finally becoming widely known.

Sweelinck, Jan Pieterszoon, b. 1562, Deventer—d. 1621, Amsterdam. Most prominent Dutch composer, organist, teacher. His organ technique, especially his independent treatment of the pedal, had deep influence on an entire generation of European instrumentalists, including Bach. As composer he was a prime developer of the fugue form.

Telemann, Georg Philipp, b. 1681, Magdeburg, Germany—d. 1767, Hamburg. One of the most versatile and prolific composers of all time; the sum of his works is larger than Bach's and Handel's put together. Wrote with remarkable facility and technical competence. His style is light, melodic, "gallant" and more French than German in flavor. Was immensely popular in his time, later his appeal declined, but today his music is again much heard and appreciated.

Tischer, Johann Nikolaus, b. 1731, (Germany)—d. 1767. A pupil of J. S. Bach, although his works show more the influence of Telemann and the "gallant" style. One of the very few eighteenth century composers who wrote keyboard music "for the young beginner".

Trabacci, Giovanni Maria, b. ca. 1580, Italy—d. 1647, Naples. Organist at the court chapel in Naples. Most notable are his instrumental compositions, often of venturesome polyphonic textures. Was killed in street fighting between Neopolitans and Spanish troops.

Walther, Johann Gottfried, b. 1684, Erfurt, Germany—d. 1748, Weimar. Highly respected organist, composer and teacher; a relative of J. S. Bach. Especially noteworthy are his chorale arrangements and variations for the organ, woven with first-rate contrapuntal artistry. He also wrote a Music Dictionary, one of the first to combine biography with definitions of musical terms.

Weckmann, Matthias, b. 1619, Oppershausen, Germany—d. 1674, Hamburg. Organist at St. James Church in Hamburg. His keyboard works mark a milestone in the development of a deeply expressive, "arioso" style in German instrumental literature of the period. Founder of a *Collegium Musicum,* one of the first of such public concert societies.

Witt, Christian Friedrich, b. 1660, Altenburg, Germany—d. 1716, Altenburg. Court composer and conductor at Gotha; significant master of the German Baroque. His Passacaglia in D minor was published, and for a long time was known as the work of J. S. Bach.

Zipoli, Domenico, b. 1688, Prato, Italy—d. 1726, Cordoba, Argentina. Famed Italian organist and composer. He studied in Naples, lived in Rome and Seville. His harpsichord music, somewhat between the styles of Pasquini and Alessandro Scarlatti, was very popular in the early eighteenth century and greatly deserves the increased interest it has been enjoying in our time. One of the first baroque musicians to emigrate to the New World, where he served as organist in the Jesuit Church of Cordoba, Argentina.

GLOSSARY

Allemande (Alman) A dance form in moderate 4/4 time, usually starting with a short up-beat. It is the first movement of the baroque suite, unless preceded by a Prelude. The term is a French word, meaning "German", but the dance itself has nothing to do with the later German Dance.

Aria Usually, the term means an elaborate vocal piece. During the Baroque it also meant a simple, song-like instrumental composition which occasionally served as the theme of a set of variations.

Ballet In the 17th century the term meant not only a staged pantomime, but also a dance suite or a single dance-like instrumental composition.

Bergamasca A lively, pastoral Italian dance. In the early Baroque it usually meant a piece in variation form, built on a tonic-subdominant-dominant-tonic harmonic sequence.

Bourrée Originally an old French folk dance. Since the 17th century it has been an optional movement in the baroque suite in lively 4/4 time, usually with an upbeat of a quarter note or two eighth notes.

Canon The most exacting polyphonic form in which a melody line sounded by one voice is strictly imitated in one or more other voices, either at the unison, at the octave, or at another chosen interval.

Canzon (Canzona, Chanson) Originally a song, a vocal piece. In the Middle-Ages the song of the troubadours; in the Renaissance a madrigal-type vocal composition. From the 16th century on it also had designated an instrumental form. Sometimes it is called Canzone da Sonar, a song to be sounded on an instrument. The Canzon is usually polyphonic in texture but has no definite form. It may also consist of several thematically related sections. It is the ancestor not only of the Ricercata and the Fugue, but also of the baroque Sonata.

Capriccio (Caprice) In general, a lively instrumental piece in free style, in which, as Rousseau says in his Dictionary of Music (1767): "the composer gives loose rein to his genius and submits himself to the fire of composition". During the Baroque the term is almost identical with the Fantasia, and in the 19th century with the Scherzo.

Carillon A percussion instrument consisting of a set of chromatically tuned bells. Also, a piece of music suggesting the sound of this instrument.

Chaconne and Passacaglia Closely related baroque instrumental forms in slow triple meter. In essence, they are both a series of variations either on a short, four to eight measure *basso ostinato* melody or on an harmonic sequence of similar length. During the early Baroque the terms were interchangeable; according to later, 18th and 19th century definitions, however, variations on a bass melody are called a Passacaglia and on a set succession of harmonies a Chaconne.

Choral Prelude Polyphonic instrumental piece, usually written for the organ, in which the main theme, a hymn, is interwoven with and surrounded by contrasting melodic passages in one or more other voices.

Courante (Coranto) A lively dance in triple time; usually the second movement of the Suite.

Divertimento During the Italian Baroque, a light instrumental composition in one or several movements. Haydn used the term as a title of some of his clavier sonatas and string quartets. Mozart wrote many Divertimenti for various small instrumental groups.

Fantasia (Fantasy) The term covers a wide variety of instrumental forms, all of which have in common a certain freedom of construction and often a quasi-improvisatory character.

Fugue (Fuga) This musical form is as characteristic of the Baroque as the Sonata is of the Classical period. In essence, the Fugue is a polyphonic piece conceived for two or more parts (voices). The voices enter successively with the same theme in alternating tonic and dominant keys (*subject* and *answer*). Each voice, after stating the subject, usually continues with different thematic material (*countersubject*) which is heard simultaneously with the entry of the subject in another voice. As a rule, the subject and countersubject appear several times in each voice during the course of the piece. Often digressing thematic passages, called *episodes*, connect the entry of themes in the different voices. The first section of the fugue, to the point where the subject has been stated once in each voice, is called the *exposition.* The fugue does not have a strict form. There can be great variety and freedom in its construction, as evidenced by the works of its unsurpassed master, J. S. Bach.

Gailliard (Galiardo) See *Pavane.*

Gavotte A graceful, old French dance in moderate 4/4 time, usually beginning on the third beat of the measure. It is an optional movement in the baroque suite and is frequently followed by a second Gavotte, called *Musette*, after which the first section is repeated.

Gigue (Giga) The last and liveliest movement of

the baroque suite, in 6/8, 9/8 or 12/8 time. Its origin is obscure. The word derives from the Italian "giga", an early fiddle, but the dance itself probably came from the *jig* a 16th century English-Scotch-Irish country dance.

Ground, Ground Bass A series of variations over a persistently repeated unchanging bass line (*basso ostinato*) usually four to eight measures in length. Closely related to the *Chaconne* and the *Passacaglia.*

Hornpipe A lively English dance during a period extending from the 16th to the 19th centuries. It derived its name from a primitive instrument—a pipe made from the horn of an animal—which often accompanied this dance.

Intonazione A prelude, usually for the organ, played before the church service.

Inventio J. S. Bach's title for his short, masterfully constructed keyboard works in imitative, two-voice counterpoint. (Bach calls the Three-Voice Inventions *Sinfonias.)*

L. An abbreviation for "Longo", Alessandro Longo, Italian pianist and editor, (1864-1945) who made a catalogue of, and numbered all Domenico Scarlatti's keyboard works.

Loure Originally, the name of an old, bagpipe-like instrument in France. As an occasional movement in the baroque suite, it is a dance form in slow or moderate 3/4 or 6/4 time with heavily accented dotted notes.

Minuet (Menuet) Graceful French dance in 3/4 time which became popular during the reign of Louis XIV mainly through the works of Lully. (The little Minuet by Lully in this volume is one of the first examples of this form.) The dance retained its popularity all through the 17th and 18th centuries. Always in triple time, originally it was of moderate tempo, stately and refined in character; as such it became part of the baroque suite around 1700. In the second half of the 18th century, in a somewhat changed form, it was incorporated into the classical sonata and symphony. With Haydn and Mozart the tempo of the Minuet became livelier, its restraint and grace often replaced by a more robust, country dance quality, akin to the Ländler. With Beethoven the tempo further quickened and the form developed into the Scherzo.

Musette An 18th century French bagpipe; a dance piece with a sustained drone bass imitating the sound of this lusty instrument. It is usually a companion piece of the Gavotte.

Ordre See *Suite.*

Partita (Partie) Another 18th century term for the Suite. Occasionally it also meant a set of variations.

Passacaglia See *Chaconne.*

Passepied An old French round-dance. During the reign of Louis XIV it was introduced into the ballet and later became an optional movement in the suite. It is in triple meter, of gay, spirited character, and it usually begins on the third beat of the measure.

Pavane A rather slow, dignified dance of Italian or Spanish origin. It was popular in the 16th century and is often found among the works of English Virginalists. The Pavane is usually followed by the *Galliard*, a gay and lively dance in triple meter.

Polonaise Polish dance of a stately, processional character, in 3/4 time. It originated in the 16th century, probably from court ceremonies and it appears frequently among the works of 18th and 19th century masters. Chopin imbued the form with an intensely lyric, and often heroic substance.

Preambulum See *Preludium.* Another name for the baroque Prelude.

Preludium (Prelude) Literally, a piece of music which serves as an introduction to another piece (such as fugue) or a group of pieces (as in the baroque suite). It is often written in a free form, in the manner of an improvisation. Since Chopin, the title Prelude is used for a short, independent composition, usually of a lyric, and sometimes of a descriptive character (Debussy).

Ricercata (Ricercare) The word comes from the Italian verb "to search out". It is a polyphonic instrumental composition in strict imitative style, a forerunner of the fugue.

Rigaudon (Rigadoon) A lively dance in 2/4 or 4/4 time, similar to the *Bourrée.* It probably originated in the South of France and is an optional movement in the baroque suite.

Rondo (Rondeau) A musical form of French origin in which a main theme (rondeau) alternates with two or more secondary themes (couplets, episodes). Its simplest pattern is A-B-A-C-A, where A represents the main theme and B and C the episodes. The first great master of this form was Couperin. As the last movement of the classical sonata, the rondo has a more rounded and cohesive construction. The favorite pattern of Mozart and Beethoven is A-B-A-C-A-B-A. There is a smooth transition between the themes; the first episode (B) which appears in the dominant key, is repeated in the main key just before the last reprise of the main theme. The middle episode (C) is often replaced by a development section.

Sarabande A stately and solemn old Spanish dance in triple meter. As a part of the baroque suite it usually serves the function of a slow movement.

Siciliano (Siciliana) An instrumental or vocal piece of pastoral character in calm, 6/8 time. It presumably derived from a Sicilian dance and was a very popular musical form during the 18th century.

Sinfonia The Italian word for Symphony. It usually denotes orchestral pieces of various kinds. J. S. Bach uses the term as the title for his Three-Voice Inventions, short, masterfully constructed keyboard works in imitative counterpoint.

Sonata One of the most important of all instrumental forms. The name derives from the Italian word *sonare*, "to sound" on an instrument, in contrast to the Cantata, which comes from *cantare,* "to sing".

There are various types of baroque sonatas differing both in the number and the construction of the movements. The earliest examples of this form closely resemble the suite. In Kuhlau's Biblical Sonatas, the first keyboard works of the genre, each movement is headed by a descriptive programmatic title. Domenico Scarlatti's sonatas, true gems of the High-Baroque, consist of one movement in binary (two-section) form. In the sonatas of Pergolesi, Paradisi, Galuppi, and Kirnberger the polythematic character of the first movement and other architectural features of the later, full sonata are more and more discernible. The Clavier sonatas of C. P. E. Bach are in three movements, fast-slow-fast, and lead directly to Haydn, Mozart and the supreme master of the form, Beethoven.

The classical sonata usually consists of four movements: Allegro—Adagio or Andante—Minuet or Scherzo—Finale (Rondo). Occasionally the Minuet or the Adagio is omitted. The first movement is written in the sonata form, proper, often referred to as the Sonata Allegro form. This consists of three sections: *exposition, development* and *recapitulation.* The exposition introduces the main building blocks of the form, two or three contrasting themes, connected by transitory passages and ending in the dominant key (or in the parallel major, if the main theme is in a minor key). The development section further expands, develops these themes, or fragments thereof, in a great variety of ways. This section is usually very modulatory in character and tends to create a feeling of tension, leading to a climactic point. The recapitulation is basically a re-statement of the exposition, with certain changes to bring the movement to a close in the "home" key.

Sonatas of the romantic and contemporary literature tend to deviate from the above pattern. They are more free, and often more fantasy-like in construction, although in most cases they still retain certain elements, especially the architectural logic of this indestructible form.

Suite, Partita, Partie, Ordre One of the most important instrumental forms of the baroque era. It is a set of contrasting, stylized dance movements, usually all in the same key. Most often it consists of the *Allemande, Courante, Sarabande, Gigue,* in that order. Occasionally the set is preceded by a *Prelude* and frequently there are other dance movements, such as the *Minuet, Gavotte, Bourrée,* and *Passepied* interpolated between the Sarabande and Gigue.

Toccata A free-style keyboard piece, usually in rapid tempo. The word comes from the Italian *toccare*, "to touch", implying a certain lightness and brilliance in execution.

Villanella Rustic, lighthearted Italian dance song of the 16th and 17th centuries. A brief instrumental piece of happy, carefree character.